94¢

D0878128

SPECTACULAR
CHESS PROBLEMS

200 GEMS BY AMERICAN COMPOSERS

selected by
KENNETH S. HOWARD

Second Edition

DOVER PUBLICATIONS, INC., NEW YORK

Published in Canada by General Publishing Company, Ltd., 30 Lesmill Road, Don Mills, Toronto, Ontario.
Published in the United Kingdom by Constable and Company, Ltd., 10 Orange Street, London WC 2.

Spectacular Chess Problems is a new work, first published by Dover Publications, Inc., in 1965.

Standard Book Number: 486-21477-X
Library of Congress Catalog Card Number: 68-13319

Manufactured in the United States of America
Dover Publications, Inc.
180 Varick Street
New York, N.Y. 10014

Note to the Second Edition

THREE of the problems in the first edition have been replaced with other problems in this edition and a number of inaccuracies corrected.

K. S. H.

Dover, New Jersey
September, 1967

Contents

Introduction

THERE IS a basic distinction between a chess endgame and a problem. In both, conventionally, white moves first. In the endgame a win—or draw—by white, against black's superior or equal force, has to be demonstrated in an indefinite number of moves. In the problem, on the other hand, white must mate black in a *specified* number of moves.

While the initial positions in endgames are frequently similar to those that arise in actual games, those in most problems would never be found in over-the-board play. The chess problem is a position composed to illustrate some interesting strategic or artistic idea, and in the majority of cases has a much more involved arrangement of men than ever would occur in a game; the only convention that always must be observed in composing an *orthodox* problem being that the position must be one which could be reached in a game, however unnatural the play leading to it.

Like the game itself, the composing of chess problems dates from the Middle Ages, and in earlier times there was less differentiation between the endgame and the problem. In fact, until the development of the modern problem, it was considered desirable for problems to have a gamelike appearance and men that took no part in the play were often added to make the opposing forces seem more equal.

Comparatively little attention was given to problem composition in the United States prior to the time that Paul Morphy's meteoric achievements, a century ago, aroused wide interest in chess throughout the country. Chess columns began to appear in newspapers, and Miron J. Hazeltine's famous column in the *New York Clipper,* started in 1856, continued for nearly half a century.

Born in 1841, four years younger than Morphy, Sam Loyd began to compose in his early teens, while Eugene B. Cook, eleven years older than Loyd, had begun composing by the time he was twenty. With a group of other problemists they pioneered the development of the chess problem in America.

Spectacular Chess

IN PREPARING this volume the author's aim has been to provide simple entertainment, rather than instruction in the intricacies of chess problem composition. To most problem fans, who look upon problem solving chiefly as a pleasant pastime, the striking keymove, the subtle mainplay, or some unexpected maneuver, has the greatest appeal.

So in presenting this collection of problems by American composers, he has selected compositions which he believes will charm the solver who solves primarily for enjoyment, and who may have little interest in the complexities of involved themes that may only be appreciated by students of problem construction.

The collection does not pretend to be representative of the works of all leading American composers; prize-winning positions have not been included merely because they have been honored in tourneys, many famed compositions being omitted; and examples of various strategic maneuvers have been selected chiefly where they have some spectacular keymove or unusual continuations. Some of the positions may be solved quite readily; a few may prove decidedly baffling and require extensive analysis.

Lightweight positions usually look the most inviting to the fan who is solving as a diversion, although ofttimes they are more difficult to solve than problems with many men, because they frequently offer fewer guideposts to the solver. Over one-half of the positions chosen have twelve or less men, forty of them being *miniatures*, with seven or fewer men.

So-called *task problems* have not been included merely because some ingenious problemist has successfully achieved a particular task, perhaps the "ultimate setting." Several examples, however, which the author believes will especially delight the solver, have been selected.

With an unfortunately aggressive key, No. 31 features the promotion of a white pawn to each of four different white pieces according to black's moves. The same task, with a better key and a more economical setting, was shown by Wurzburg in No. 95, thirty years later.

Problems No. 1 and No. 87 show two consecutive promotions of pawns to bishops, while No. 91 has three. No. 121 has promotions of a pawn to queen and to knight on three different squares, according to black's play.

Among other problems regarded as task compositions, there may be included No. 74, called the "Queen's Cross," where the twelve different squares from which the queen delivers mate form a cross on the chessboard; No. 114 where two black knights self-block the black king on four squares; and No. 108 where a white rook forms an *ambush* below three white pawns. In No. 80 there are seven different captures of a white bishop that defeat the threatened mate.

In a number of problems the key permits the white king to be checked, sometimes in several ways, and in Nos. 30, 66, and 106 it submits him to double check. In a couple of problems, Nos. 105 and 192, one king mates the other by discovered checks.

Although difficulty of solution may only be one of the meritorious features of a modern chess problem, yet to most solvers a chess problem is still primarily a *problem,* and a subtle solution is always appreciated.

Loyd's No. 12 was composed specifically to prove difficult to solve. In reproducing it in his *Het Schaakprobleem (The Chess Problem),* Weenink comments: "The key is the most baffling that could be imagined." The entire mainplay needs to be envisioned before the reason for the keymove becomes apparent.

The keys and mainplays in Wash's No. 37 and No. 38 are similarly obscure. Then coming down to more recent days, both in Berd's No. 186 and No. 189 there is an unusually well hidden second-move continuation, the *raison d'être* for the composition.

Some of the positions, such as No. 25 and No. 130, merely illustrate a single whimsical idea. Finally, many of the problems owe their attractiveness to the repetition, or *echoing,* of some particular line of play or of some pleasing mating position.

The solver, who is desirous of acquiring any real degree of skill, should practice solving directly from diagrammed positions, rather than by setting up the problems on a chessboard. In the game itself a player is not permitted to move the men about, but is obliged to visualize the possibilities following his choice of moves. The same procedure should be followed in solving problems. When a solver, after a little practice, learns to move the men in his "mind's eye," he actually may find it easier to do so when looking at a diagram than if the position were set up on a board.

A further advantage of learning to solve from the diagram is that the problem fan will be able to study problems at many times and places where no board and men are available, or even where a pocket board may not be convenient to use.

* * * * *

The problems in the following pages are arranged in an approximately chronological order, according to their first publication, although in some instances the exact dates have been difficult to ascertain.

The symbol V indicates that the position is a revised *version* of the problem as initially published, having been altered either because the original position was found to be unsound or to incorporate some improvement.

Some of the problems were published posthumously. No. 103 and No. 104 by Ben S. Wash were included in Alain White's *The White King,* printed in 1914, although they may have been published elsewhere previously. No. 169 is from a manuscript collection of Dr. Dobbs' compositions; and Nos. 193, 194, 195, 196 and 199 were taken by Edgar Holladay, problem editor of the American Chess Bulletin, from a manuscript collection left by Otto Wurzburg.

In each problem white moves first and must mate in the stipulated number of moves.

The solutions to the problems, in most instances, are given in considerable detail to make certain that interesting continuations will not be overlooked.

The collection comprises 47 two-movers, 122 three-movers, 29 four-movers and two five-move problems.

The Problems

1

EUGENE B. COOK
Illustrated London News
January 6, 1855

White mates in three moves

2

EUGENE B. COOK
New York Albion
October 20, 1855

White mates in four moves

3

SAMUEL LOYD
First Prize
Chess Monthly
1857

White mates in three moves

4

SAMUEL LOYD
First Prize
New York Albion
August 7, 1858

White mates in three moves

5

SAMUEL LOYD
Cincinnati Dispatch
September 5, 1858

White mates in three moves

6

SAMUEL LOYD
V   First Prize
American Union
October, 1858

White mates in three moves

7

SAMUEL LOYD
Syracuse Standard
circa 1858

White mates in three moves

8

GEORGE N. CHENEY
circa 1858

White mates in four moves

9

SAMUEL LOYD
Frank Leslie's Magazine
February 12, 1859

White mates in three moves

10

GEORGE N. CHENEY
Brooklyn Standard
November, 1860

White mates in three moves

11

SAMUEL LOYD
La Stratégie
June 15, 1867

White mates in three moves

12

SAMUEL LOYD
Second Prize Set
Paris Tourney
1867

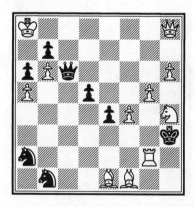

White mates in four moves

13

SAMUEL LOYD
V Second Prize Set
Paris Tourney
1867

White mates in five moves

14

EUGENE B. COOK
American Chess Nuts
1868

White mates in four moves

15

GEORGE N. CHENEY
American Chess Nuts
1868

White mates in four moves

16

SAMUEL LOYD
Leipziger Illustrirte Zeitung
October 23, 1869

White mates in three moves

17

WILLIAM MEREDITH
Dubuque Chess Journal
June, 1873

White mates in two moves

18

WILLIAM A. SHINKMAN
Western Advertiser
1873

White mates in three moves

19

WILLIAM A. SHINKMAN
V   *Chess Record*
May, 1874

White mates in two moves

20

WILLIAM MEREDITH
Maryland Chess Review
December, 1874

White mates in two moves

21

WILLIAM A. SHINKMAN
Deutsche Schachzeitung
March, 1875

White mates in three moves

22

SAMUEL LOYD
Cleveland Leader
1876

White mates in three moves

23

SAMUEL LOYD
Detroit Free Press
January, 1877

White mates in three moves

24

SAMUEL LOYD
Centennial Congress
Problem Tourney
1877

White mates in four moves

25

SAMUEL LOYD
Holyoke Transcript
1877

White mates in three moves

26

WILLIAM A. SHINKMAN
American Chess Journal
May, 1878

White mates in three moves

27

SAMUEL LOYD
First Prize
American Chess and
Problem Association
Turf, Field and Farm
1878

White mates in four moves

28

C. C. MOORE
Cleveland Voice Tourney
1878

White mates in four moves

29

BENJAMIN S. WASH
Honorable Mention
Huddersfield College Magazine
Tourney
1879–1880

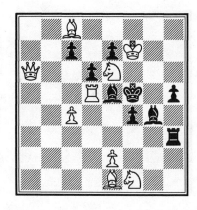

White mates in three moves

30

HENRY, EDGAR and
JACOB BETTMANN
Quebec Chronicle
August 25, 1882

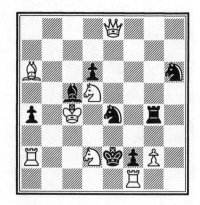

White mates in two moves

31

WILLIAM A. SHINKMAN
Detroit Free Press
December 22, 1883

White mates in three moves

32

JOSEPH C. J. WAINWRIGHT
Mirror of American Sports
1884

White mates in three moves

33

WILLIAM A. SHINKMAN
Chess Monthly Tourney
May, 1885

White mates in two moves

34

WILLIAM A. SHINKMAN
V   *Detroit Free Press*
1885

White mates in three moves

35

WILLIAM A. SHINKMAN
Detroit Free Press
1885

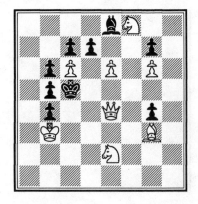

White mates in two moves

36

JOSEPH C. J. WAINWRIGHT
First Prize
Mirror of American Sports
1885

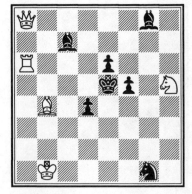

White mates in three moves

37

BENJAMIN S. WASH
circa 1885

White mates in four moves

38

BENJAMIN S. WASH
circa 1885

White mates in four moves

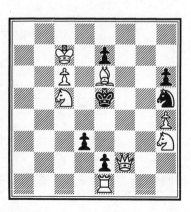

39

WILLIAM A. SHINKMAN
circa 1885

White mates in two moves

40

WILLIAM MEREDITH
Dubuque Chess Journal
November, 1886

White mates in two moves

41

WILLIAM MEREDITH
Dubuque Chess Journal
December, 1886

White mates in two moves

42

DAVID T. BROCK
Columbia Chess Chronicle
December 24, 1887

White mates in four moves

43

HENRY and EDGAR
BETTMANN
Second Prize
Nashville American
1887

White mates in two moves

44

LOUIS H. JOKISCH
Nashville American
March, 1888

White mates in three moves

45

WILLIAM A. SHINKMAN
Yenowine News
April 15, 1888

White mates in three moves

46

WILLIAM MEREDITH
Dubuque Chess Journal
August, 1888

White mates in three moves

47

WILLIAM MEREDITH
First Prize
Ninth Tourney
Dubuque Chess Journal
December, 1889

White mates in two moves

48

WILLIAM A. SHINKMAN
Dubuque Chess Journal
November, 1890

White mates in three moves

49

WILLIAM A. SHINKMAN
First Prize
St. John's Globe
1890

White mates in three moves

50

JOSEPH C. J. WAINWRIGHT
Jamaica Gleaner
1890

White mates in three moves

51

SAMUEL LOYD
New York State
Chess Association
February 22, 1892

White mates in two moves

52

WILLIAM A. SHINKMAN
Baltimore News
1892

White mates in three moves

53

WILLIAM A. SHINKMAN
Deutsche Schachzeitung
September, 1893

White mates in four moves

54

OTTO WURZBURG
V   *Bahn Frei*
1895

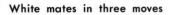

White mates in three moves

55

SAMUEL LOYD
New York Commercial Advertiser
1897

White mates in two moves

56

OTTO WURZBURG
American Chess Magazine
1898

White mates in three moves

57

JOSEPH C. J. WAINWRIGHT
The Boston Post
August, 1901

White mates in three moves

58

WILLIAM A. SHINKMAN
V   *British Chess Magazine*
October, 1901

White mates in three moves

59

WILLIAM A. SHINKMAN
Schachminiaturen
1901

White mates in three moves

60

WILLIAM A. SHINKMAN
V   *Schachminiaturen*
1901.

White mates in four moves

61

JOSEPH C. J. WAINWRIGHT
Checkmate
1901

White mates in four moves

62

JOSEPH C. J. WAINWRIGHT
Checkmate
1901

White mates in four moves

63

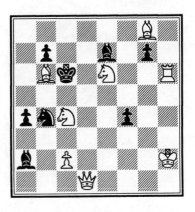

HENRY W. BARRY
First Prize
La Stratégie
November, 1901

White mates in two moves

64

WILLIAM A. SHINKMAN
Checkmate
February, 1903

White mates in two moves

65

WILLIAM A. SHINKMAN
Checkmate
July, 1903

White mates in three moves

66

SAMUEL LOYD
First Prize
Checkmate
1903

White mates in three moves

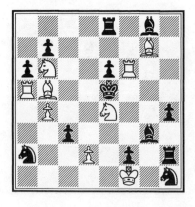

67

WILLIAM A. SHINKMAN
The Corsair
February 29, 1904

White mates in four moves

68

WALTER I. KENNARD
Checkmate
1904

White mates in two moves

69

WALTER I. KENNARD
Checkmate
1904

White mates in two moves

70

WILLIAM A. SHINKMAN
Lasker's Chess Magazine
June , 1905

White mates in five moves

71

WILLIAM A. SHINKMAN
V *Wiener Schachzeitung*
1905

White mates in three moves

72

MURRAY MARBLE
Lasker's Chess Magazine
September, 1906

White mates in three moves

73

FREDERICK GAMAGE
Tidskrift för Schack
July–August, 1905

White mates in three moves

74

JOSEPH C. J. WAINWRIGHT
Les Tours de Force
1906

White mates in two moves

75

WILLIAM A. SHINKMAN
Neues Wiener Tageblatt
February 28, 1908

White mates in three moves

76

FREDERICK GAMAGE
Lasker's Chess Magazine
1908

White mates in three moves

77

OTTO WURZBURG
V   *Zlata Praha*
June 25, 1909

White mates in three moves

78

MURRAY MARBLE
Indian Field
1909

White mates in three moves

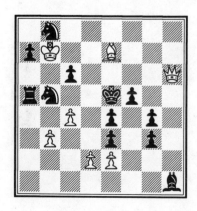

79

LOUIS H. JOKISCH
Tidskrift för Schack
1909

White mates in two moves

80

MURRAY MARBLE
First Prize
La Stratégie
1909

White mates in two moves

81

WILLIAM A. SHINKMAN
The White Rooks
1910

White mates in three moves

82

JOSEPH C. J. WAINWRIGHT
American Chess Bulletin
February, 1911

White mates in three moves

83

OTTO WURZBURG
Deutsches Wochenschach
1911

White mates in four moves

84

EUGENE B. COOK
More White Rooks
1911

White mates in three moves

85

HENRY WALD BETTMANN
More White Rooks
1911

White mates in three moves

86

ALAIN WHITE
(after A. Arnell)
More White Rooks
1911

White mates in four moves

87

GEORGE E. CARPENTER
Westen und Daheim
1911

White mates in three moves

88

FREDERICK GAMAGE
First Prize
Tidskrift för Schack
1911

White mates in two moves

89

ALAIN WHITE
Running the Gauntlet
1911

White mates in three moves

90

OTTO WURZBURG
Westen und Daheim
September 15, 1912

White mates in three moves

91

HENRY WALD BETTMANN
The Theory of Pawn Promotion
1912

White mates in four moves

92

WILLIAM A. SHINKMAN
La Stratêgie
January, 1913

White mates in three moves

93

OTTO WURZBURG
First Prize
Samuel Loyd Memorial Tourney
1913

White mates in three moves

94

DARSO J. DENSMORE
First Prize
Brooklyn Chess Club Tourney
1913–1914

White mates in three moves

95

OTTO WURZBURG
(after Niels Hoeg)
The Pittsburgh Gazette-Times
January 4, 1914

White mates in three moves

96

WILLIAM B. RICE
The Hampshire Telegraph
April 3, 1914

White mates in three moves

97

OTTO WURZBURG
The Problem
April 18, 1914

White mates in three moves

98

OTTO WURZBURG
Der Westen
April 19, 1914

White mates in three moves

99

DARSO J. DENSMORE
The Problem
September 19, 1914

White mates in three moves

100

FREDERICK GAMAGE
First Prize
Tidskrift för Schack
September, 1914

White mates in two moves

101

GILBERT DOBBS
Tidskrift för Schack
1914

White mates in three moves

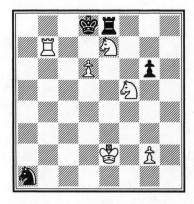

102

OTTO WURZBURG
The Problem
1914

White mates in three moves

103

BENJAMIN S. WASH
The White King
1914

White mates in three moves

104

BENJAMIN S. WASH
The White King
1914

White mates in three moves

105

GEORGE E. CARPENTER
The White King
1914

White mates in three moves

106

HENRY WALD BETTMANN
The White King
1914

White mates in four moves

107

CHARLES PROMISLO
First Honorable Mention
Good Companions
February 22, 1915

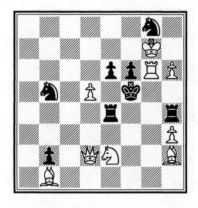

White mates in two moves

108

WALTER I. KENNARD
American Chess Bulletin
December, 1915

White mates in four moves

109

WILLIAM A. SHINKMAN
Tasks and Echoes
1915

White mates in three moves

110

DARSO J. DENSMORE
January 12, 1916

White mates in three moves

111

DARSO J. DENSMORE
V   *The Pittsburgh Gazette-Times*
February 27, 1916

White mates in three moves

112

WILLIAM A. SHINKMAN
First Prize in Theme Contest
The Pittsburgh Gazette-Times
June 25, 1916

White mates in three moves

113

LOUIS ROTHSTEIN
The Pittsburgh Gazette-Times
May 20, 1917

White mates in three moves

114

FRANK JANET
The Chess Amateur
May, 1918

White mates in two moves

115

ALAIN WHITE
First Prize
Seventh Meredith Tourney
Good Companions
May, 1918

White mates in two moves

116

WILLIAM A. SHINKMAN
and OTTO WURZBURG
First Prize Class B
Densmore Memorial Tourney
1918

White mates in three moves

117

GILBERT DOBBS
American Chess Bulletin
1919

White mates in three moves

118

CHARLES PROMISLO
Second Prize
The Boston Transcript
1919

White mates in two moves

119

HENRY WALD BETTMANN
Good Companions
April, 1921

White mates in two moves

120

CHARLES PROMISLO
Third Honorable Mention
Meredith Section
Eighth American Chess Congress
August, 1921

White mates in two moves

121

HENRY WALD BETTMANN
Good Companions
January, 1923

White mates in two moves

122

KENNETH S. HOWARD
American Chess Bulletin
September–October, 1925

White mates in three moves

123

KENNETH S. HOWARD
First Honorable Mention
Twelfth Informal Tourney
The Weekly Westminster
January 16, 1926

White mates in four moves

124

KENNETH S. HOWARD
The Observer
April 25, 1926

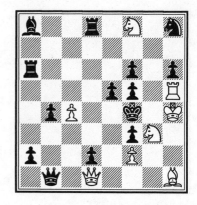

White mates in three moves

125

KENNETH S. HOWARD
The Pittsburgh Post
July 11, 1926

White mates in four moves

126

KENNETH S. HOWARD
The Weekly Westminster
August 14, 1926

White mates in four moves

127

OTTO WURZBURG
Fourth Prize
Prager Presse
1926

White mates in three moves

128

KENNETH S. HOWARD
American Chess Bulletin
February, 1927

White mates in four moves

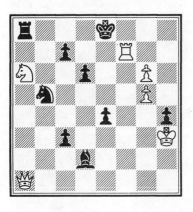

129

KENNETH S. HOWARD
V *The Observer*
June 29, 1930

White mates in three moves

130

KENNETH S. HOWARD
Skakbladet
July, 1930

White mates in three moves

131

KENNETH S. HOWARD
Grand Rapids Herald
December 3, 1933

White mates in two moves

132

GILBERT DOBBS
Chess Review
1933

White mates in three moves

133

KENNETH S. HOWARD
Skakbladet
April, 1934

White mates in two moves

134

GILBERT DOBBS
The Cincinnati Enquirer
1934

White mates in three moves

135

WALTER JACOBS
British Chess Magazine
March, 1935

White mates in three moves

136

KENNETH S. HOWARD
American Chess Bulletin
December, 1935

White mates in four moves

137

GEOFFREY MOTT-SMITH
Chess Review
1935

White mates in two moves

138

WALTER JACOBS
Chess Review
1935

White mates in three moves

139

GILBERT DOBBS
Third Prize
First Cheney Miniature Tourney
1935

White mates in three moves

140

OTTO WURZBURG
American Chess Bulletin
January, 1936

White mates in two moves

141

KENNETH S. HOWARD
Second and Third Honorable
Mention (ex aequo)
Informal Tourney
The Western Morning News
January–June, 1936

White mates in three moves

142

ALEXANDER KISH
American Chess Bulletin
May–June, 1936

White mates in two moves

143

OTTO WURZBURG
American Chess Bulletin
July–August, 1936

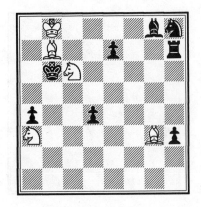

White mates in three moves

144

VINCENT L. EATON
Entry in Tourney No. 20
British Chess Federation
1936

White mates in three moves

145

VINCENT L. EATON
Melbourne Leader
1936

White mates in two moves

146

GILBERT DOBBS
The Problemist
1937

White mates in three moves

147

OTTO WURZBURG
First Prize
Third Cheney Miniature Tourney
1937

White mates in four moves

148

VINCENT L. EATON
Second Prize
17th International Tourney
Skakbladet
1937

White mates in three moves

149

WILLIAM B. RICE
The Emery Memorial
1937

White mates in three moves

150

MAXWELL BUKOFZER
The Emery Memorial
1937

White mates in four moves

KENNETH S. HOWARD
American Chess Bulletin
May–June, 1938

White mates in three moves

KENNETH S. HOWARD
American Chess Bulletin
July–August, 1938

White mates in three moves

GILBERT DOBBS
Honorable Mention
Fourth Cheney Miniature Tourney
1938

White mates in three moves

154

OTTO WURZBURG
American Chess Bulletin
May–June, 1939

White mates in three moves

155

GILBERT DOBBS
British Chess Magazine
July, 1939

White mates in three moves

156

OTTO WURZBURG
The Atlanta Journal
September 29, 1939

White mates in two moves

157

WILLIAM A. BEERS
First Prize
American Chess Bulletin
1939

White mates in two moves

158

OTTO WURZBURG
First Prize
American Chess Bulletin
1939

White mates in three moves

159

GILBERT DOBBS
First Honorable Mention
American Chess Bulletin
1939

White mates in three moves

160

GEOFFREY MOTT-SMITH
Chess Review
1939

White mates in two moves

161

E. NEUHAUS, JR.
American Chess Bulletin
September–October, 1940

White mates in two moves

162

FREDERICK GAMAGE
First Prize
John Keeble Memorial Tourney
The Falkirk Herald
1940

White mates in two moves

163

FREDERICK GAMAGE
First Prize
American Chess Bulletin
1940

White mates in two moves

164

WALTER JACOBS
First Prize
American Chess Bulletin
1940

White mates in three moves

165

OTTO WURZBURG
First Honorable Mention
American Chess Bulletin
1940

White mates in three moves

166

ALAIN WHITE
American Chess Bulletin
November–December, 1941

White mates in two moves

167

FREDERICK GAMAGE
First Prize
Meredith Tourney
The Chess Correspondent
November, 1941

White mates in two moves

168

WALTER JACOBS
First Prize
American Chess Bulletin
1941

White mates in three moves

169

GILBERT DOBBS
American Chess Bulletin
March–April, 1942

White mates in four moves

170

WALTER JACOBS
American Chess Bulletin
September–October, 1942

White mates in three moves

171

OTTO WURZBURG
First Prize
Sam Loyd Memorial Tourney
Chess Review
1942

White mates in three moves

172

WALTER JACOBS
First Prize
American Chess Bulletin
1942

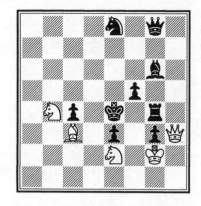

White mates in three moves

173

GEORGE W. HARGREAVES
First Honorable Mention
American Chess Bulletin
1943

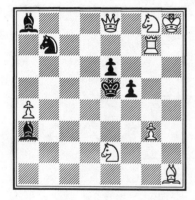

White mates in three moves

174

OTTO WURZBURG
Second Commended
American Chess Bulletin
1943

White mates in three moves

175

WALTER JACOBS
First Prize
American Chess Bulletin
1944

White mates in two moves

176

OTTO WURZBURG
Second Honorable Mention
American Chess Bulletin
1944

White mates in three moves

177

OTTO WURZBURG
First Commended
American Chess Bulletin
1944

White mates in three moves

178

KENNETH S. HOWARD
V   *British Chess Magazine*
    September, 1944

White mates in three moves

179

ERIC M. HASSBERG
New York Post
April 21, 1945

White mates in two moves

180

OTTO WURZBURG
First Honorable Mention
American Chess Bulletin
1945

White mates in three moves

181

OTTO WURZBURG
Second Honorable Mention
American Chess Bulletin
1945

White mates in three moves

182

KENNETH S. HOWARD
To Alain White
(65th Birthday Book)
1945

White mates in three moves

183

JULIUS BUCHWALD
First Prize
American Chess Bulletin
1946

White mates in two moves

184

H. M. HUSE
First Honorable Mention
American Chess Bulletin
1946

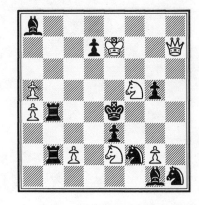

White mates in three moves

185

HAROLD BRANTON
American Chess Bulletin
May–June, 1947

White mates in three moves

186

B. M. BERD
Second Commended
American Chess Bulletin
1947

White mates in three moves

187

OTTO WURZBURG
First Prize
American Chess Bulletin
1947

White mates in three moves

188

JULIUS BUCHWALD
Third Commended
American Chess Bulletin
1948

White mates in three moves

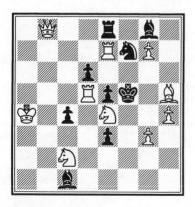

189

B. M. BERD
Fourth Commended
American Chess Bulletin
1948

White mates in three moves

190

NATHAN RUBENS
American Chess Bulletin
September–October, 1949

White mates in three moves

191

ANTONIO BELLAS
Honorable Mention
American Chess Bulletin
1949

White mates in three moves

192

NATHAN RUBENS
American Chess Bulletin
March–April, 1953

White mates in three moves

193

OTTO WURZBURG
American Chess Bulletin
May–June, 1955

White mates in three moves

194

OTTO WURZBURG
American Chess Bulletin
July–August, 1955

White mates in three moves

195

OTTO WURZBURG
Honorable Mention
American Chess Bulletin
1955

White mates in three moves

196

OTTO WURZBURG
American Chess Bulletin
November–December, 1955

White mates in three moves

197

VINCENT L. EATON
Second Prize
American Chess Bulletin
1958

White mates in three moves

198

ANTHONY TAFFS
American Chess Bulletin
November–December, 1958

White mates in three moves

199

OTTO WURZBURG
(V   *The Pittsburgh Post*)
American Chess Bulletin
September–October, 1959

White mates in three moves

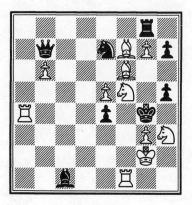

200

EDGAR HOLLADAY
Second Prize
Fortieth Anniversary Tourney
British Chess Problem Society
1960

White mates in two moves

Notation

The notation employed in giving the solutions on the following pages is the *algebraic,* a modified form of what is sometimes called the *Continental* because of its use in many European countries. It is commonly used in books on problems since it is more concise and precise than the English notation.

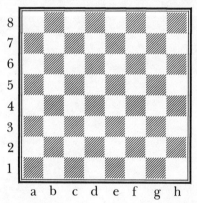

In the algebraic notation the location and moves of the men are always read from the White side of the board, or the lower side of the diagram. The files are designated "a" to "h" from left to right, and the ranks are numbered "1" to "8" reading up. Thus White's queen's rook's square is "a1" and Black's king's rook's square is "h8."

The same letters are used for the men as in the English notation with the exception of S (German *Springer*) for knight. 0-0 indicates castling with king's rook, 0-0-0 castling with queen's rook. The symbol x is used for captures and the symbol ( ) for promotion of a pawn to a piece.

The solver will find the algebraic notation not only easy to learn, but that it avoids the ambiguities and mistakes that sometimes result from the use of the English notation, where the solver must count the ranks from one side of the diagram for White's moves and from the opposite side for Black's.

Solutions and Notes

Solutions and Notes

No. 1
  1 Pe8(B), Ke6; 2 Pf8(B), Kf5; 3 Bd7

No. 2
  1 Ke2, Pg2; 2 Bf4 ck (threat), KxQB; 3 Qd2 ck, Ke5; 4 Qd6
  RxQ dbl ck; 2 Kf3, Be2 ck; 3 Ke3, any; 4 Bf4
  Rb7 dis ck; 2 Ke3, RxS; 3 Pc4 dis ck, KxB; 4 QxPf6
  Rb3 dis ck; 2 Ke3 etc.
Compare this problem with No. 66 by Loyd.

No. 3
  1 Sg4 ck, Kh1; 2 Qh2 ck, PxQ; 3 Sf2
              Kh3; 2 Sh2, Pf3; 3 Rh8
                   else; 3 Qh8
              Kf1; 2 Ra8, any; 3 Ra1
              Kf3; 2 Qc2, Pg2; 3 Qd3

When the author was twelve years old he read an article on
chess in the *American Encyclopedia,* at the conclusion of which
two positions were given as illustrations of chess problems, the
first he ever saw. One was a two-move problem by Cook, with
a waiting-move key, and the other this problem by Loyd,
which as a boy he never solved, since he did not see the continuation after 1 − − Kh1.

In the early days of problem composition it was not un-
common for problems to have checking keymoves; this position being a typical example. Any legitimate move may be
employed as the key of a problem, but as the art of problem
composition became more refined, the use of checks or of
captures of black pieces as keys was abandoned as being too
aggressive.

Sam Loyd, as he was popularly known, was born in 1841
and actually composed the majority of his chess problems before he was twenty. He was again somewhat active in problem composition in the late eighteen-seventies, but after that
only composed occasionally, No. 66 being one of his last
compositions. His principal activities were in journalistic

work and the devising of puzzles, for which he became world famous as "The Puzzle King."

No. 4

This is a waiting-move problem; White having no mating continuations until after Black moves.

1 Ba4, Rh1; 2 Sg6 ck, Kd5; 3 Sc7. This variation shows the point of the key, to guard c6.

        Bb6; 2 Sd6, any; 3 SxPc4
        Bb8; 2 Sd4 threat 3 Sc6
                 PxS; 3 BPxP
        Sb8; 2 Sd6, any; 3 SxPc4
        S else; 2 SxB, any; 3 Sc6
        QB any; 2 Sd6 etc.

No. 5

1 Ba8 threat 2 Qb7, any; 3 Qh1
        S any; 2 Qb6 (x) etc.
        Pf4; 2 Qg6 etc.
        Kf1; 2 QxP ck etc.

No. 6

1 Kd2 threat 2 Bg4 ck, SxB; 3 Rh5
        Q checks; 2 KxQ or SxQ, Bg8; 3 Bg6
                 else; 3 Pc8(Q)

No. 7

1 Bb8, Bc2, b1; 2 Pd4 ck, PxPep; 3 Se4
        Bd3; 2 Ke5 etc.
        Sd5 ck; 2 Ke5 etc.
        Sd3; 2 Ke7 etc.

No. 8

1 Sa1, Ba2; 2 Pb4 ck, PxPep; 3 Kb2, Bb1; 4 SxP
                               Sd4; 4 PxS
                            S else; 4 Pd4
        Bb3; 2 SxB ck, PxS; 3 Kd2 etc.

No. 9

1 Kc2, KxP dis ck; 2 Sc3, Kc4; 3 Qf4
                          K else; 3 QxR
        Kb5 dis ck; 2 Kb3 etc.
        R moves; 2 Sb2 ck etc.

No. 10

1 Ba8, PxP; 2 Kb7, Kd5; 3 Rd3
        Pf4; 2 Be4, any; 3 Rd3

No. 11

    1 Pa8(B), Kf8; 2 Pb8(Q) ck, Kf7; 3 Bd5
                 Ke8; 2 Ke6 etc.
                 Kg8; 2 Kg6 etc.

No. 12

With a most unexpected key and bizarre mainplay, this problem was composed specifically to baffle the solver.

    1 BxP threat 2 BxP threat 3 Qc8 ck, QxQ ck; 4 BxQ
                             QxB ck; 3 KxQ, any; 4 Qc8
        PxB dis ck; 2 Pb7 threat 3 Qc8 ck etc.
        Qc5; 2 Qe8, Qc6; 3 QxQ etc.
        Qc2; 2 Be2, QxB; 3 Qc8 ck etc.

No. 13

    1 Rf8, SxR; 2 Bf5, S any; 3 BxS, B any; 4 P moves;
                             5 B mates
        Sf4; 2 RxS etc.
        Sh4; 2 Ke2 etc.

No. 14

    1 Rf6, Pa6; 2 Ba7, Pe2; 3 Rb6, Kd4; 4 Rb3
           Pe2; 2 Bg1, Pa6; 3 Rf2, Kd4; 4 Rf3

In 1859 Loyd and Cook planned to issue a book containing a thousand problems by American composers. It was nine years later, however, before the volume, with the collaboration of William R. Henry and Charles A. Gilberg, was completed and published under the title *American Chess Nuts*. The number of problems had been increased to some twenty-four hundred, and included the works of 231 composers, Loyd contributing 353 problems and Cook 326.

Eugene B. Cook (1830-1915) had an outstanding reputation as a solver and for his ability to detect any flaw in a composition. While the origin of the term "cook," designating a second solution to a problem, thus ruining its value, is not known, it has been suggested that it may have come from Cook's remarkable accuracy as an analyst.

No. 15

    1 Qh8 threats 2 Qa1 ck or 2 Qd4 ck etc.
             Pc1(S); 2 Qb2, Pf1(S); 3 Qd2 ck, SxQ; 4 Se3

No. 16
    1 Qf1, Bb2; 2 Qb1 threat 3 QxP
                        Pg6; 3 QxB
              Bc3, d4; 2 Qd3 etc.
              Be5, f6; 2 Qf5 etc.
              Ph6; 2 Qb1 etc.
              Pg3; 2 Sg6 ck, PxS; 3 Qh3

No. 17
    1 Qh8 threat 2 Qh7
              BxR; 2 Qa8
              SxR; 2 Qh1
              SxB; 2 Qd4

William Meredith, who was born in Philadelphia in 1835, composed less than two hundred problems. Since the majority of them appeared in a single publication, Brownson's *Dubuque Chess Journal,* his work did not attain any wide recognition before his death in 1903.

Meredith's compositions were notable for their artistic and economical construction, and Alain White published a selection of them as the 1916 volume of his *Christmas Series,* with comments on the individual problems by members of the Good Companion Chess Problem Club.

Two-movers with twelve or less men came to be known as *Merediths* and the Good Companions conducted many *Meredith* tourneys for such problems. The term has since come into common usage in the problemist's vocabulary.

No. 18
    1 Pe8(R), KxP; 2 Pa8(S), Kb5; 3 Re5
              Kc5; 2 Pa8(Q), Kd6; 3 Qc6

William A. Shinkman, born in Bohemia in 1847, came to Grand Rapids, Michigan, in 1854 and lived there until his death in 1933. He began problem composition about 1870 and continued to compose throughout his life, being the most prolific of American composers, with an output of some thirty-five hundred problems, six hundred of which were reproduced in *The Golden Argosy,* the 1929 volume of *The Christmas Series.*

Because of his facility for securing marvelous effects with a minimum number of men, Shinkman became known as "The Wizard of Grand Rapids."

No. 19
    1 Ke6, Kc4; 2 Ke5
          Ke3; 2 Qf2
          Pc4; 2 Qa7
          Pe3; 2 Qf4

No. 20
    1 Qd8 threat 2 Se4
          KxP; 2 Se4
          RxQ; 2 SxP
          Kd4; 2 Qf6

No. 21
    1 Qd4, PxQ; 2 Rf7, any; 3 Rc7
          Kb7; 2 Rf7 ck, Ka8; 3 Qh8
                        Ka6; 3 Qa1
          Kd7; 2 Qg4 ck etc.

No. 22
This problem illustrates a maneuver to avoid the possibility of a stalemate.
    1 Ba7, Pf4; 2 Sb6, Ke3; 3 Qd3
          Ke4; 2 Qg3, Pf4; 3 QxPf4
                        Pg5; 3 Qe3

No. 23
    1 Qg3 threat 2 Qg8 etc.
          Ka6; 2 QxP, any; 3 Qb6
          Ka4; 2 Qc3, any; 3 Qb4
          Ba4; 2 QxP ck, Ka6; 3 Qb6
          Bb3; 2 QxP ck, Ka4; 3 Qa7

No. 24
    1 Qh8, Rc4 ck; 2 Kb3 dis ck etc.
          Rd3 ck; 2 Kc2 dis ck etc.

No. 25
    1 PxB(S), KxS; 2 Sb6, any; 3 Pa8(Q)

No. 26
    1 Rh4, Bg2; 2 Rf5 ck, Kg3; 3 Bf2
          Pe4; 2 Rh3 ck, Kf4; 3 Be3

No. 27
    1 Qf8, Ph3; 2 SxP, Ka2; 3 SxP ck etc.
          Kc4; 2 SxP, KxP; 3 SxP etc.
                    KxS; 3 Qc5 ck etc.
          KxB; 2 QSc2 ck, Ka2; 3 Qa3 ck etc.

No. 28
    1 Kb5, Ke4;   2 Kc4, Kf5;   3 Rf7, Ke6;   4 Kd4
                                   Kf5;   3 Kd4 etc.

No. 29
    1 Qa3 threat 2 Pe4 ck, KxP;   3 Sg5
                             PxPep;   3 Qd3
             RxQ;   2 Pe4 ck, PxPep;   3 Sg3
                                KxP;   3 Sg5
             BxP;   2 QxR ck, Bg4;   3 Qd3

Little is known of the chess activities of Ben Wash (1853-1906) as he was familiarly called. He is reputed to have composed some thousand problems, but to have lost the records of them, and less than two hundred have been preserved.

Alain White in *A Sketchbook of American Problematists* comments: "His problems, especially those in three moves, usually emphasize a single rather striking mainplay, often a strategic sacrifice or ambush, and the by-play is quite subordinate."

No. 30
    1 Qh5 waiting
        SxS dbl ck;   2 Kc3

Again quoting from the *Sketchbook*, "The prodigies of the problem world in America in the 1880's were the 'Bettmann Brothers' of Cincinnati. The name is slightly misleading, for, though there were two brothers, Edgar and Henry, the third and eldest of the Bettmanns, Jacob, was a first cousin. . . .

"The three Bettmanns appeared on the scene as boys in 1881, composing and solving both individually and jointly, so that the authorship of their different problems is sometimes not a little confusing to apportion correctly among them. Some of their works are to be credited to all three . . . others to the two brothers, Henry and Edgar . . . and a majority of the latter problems to Henry alone."

No. 31
    1 PxS ck, Kd6;   2 Pe8(R), Kc6;   3 Re6
             RxPc4;   2 Pe8(B), Ke6;   3 BxR
             Ke6;   2 Pe8(S), RxPc4;   3 BxR
                          else;   3 Re7
             Kc6;   2 Pe8(Q) ck, Kb6;   3 Qb5
                                Kd6;   3 Rd3

No. 32
    1 Pd3, Kf5; 2 Pe4 ck, PxPep; 3 Pd4
                        Pd5xP; 3 Qb5
                        Ke5; 3 Qb8
        S any; 2 Qb8 ck, Kf5; 3 Qf4(x)
        Pg3; 2 Qc1 etc.
        Kd6; 2 Qb8 ck etc.

No. 33
    1 Qg1 threat 2 QxB

This is an early example of the *block-threat*. In the initial position a mate is "set" for any move Black may make, but White cannot make any waiting move.

No. 34
    1 Qg1, Sf2; 2 KxS, Kd4; 3 Kf3
            Sg3; 2 KxS, Ke5; 3 Kf3

No. 35
    1 Qh1, PxPc6; 2 Qh5
        Pd6; 2 Bf2
        Pd5; 2 Qc1
        PxPe6; 2 SxP
        B any; 2 SxP

No. 36
    1 Rc6 threat 2 Rc5 ck, Kd6; 3 Rd5
        Kd5; 2 Rc5 dbl ck etc.
        Ke4; 2 RxP dbl ck, Kd3; 3 Qa6
        Pd3; 2 Bc3 ck etc.
        Bb6, a5; 2 Bd6 ck etc.

No. 37
    1 Bd1, RxP; 2 Sb4 ck (threat), BxS; 3 Pc4 ck, PxPep; 4 Bb3
        Rc6; 2 QxR ck, KxS; 3 Qd6 ck etc.
        Pa5; 2 QxR, KxS; 3 Qd6 ck etc.

No. 38
    1 Bb5, KRxB; 2 Se4 ck, BxS; 3 Pd4 ck, PxPep; 4 Qc1
        Ra6; 2 QxR etc.

This problem and No. 37, each featuring a single subtle line of play, are typical of Wash's style.

No. 39
    1 Rf1 threat 2 Qe3
        PxR; 2 Qb2

No. 40
1 Qb4 threats 2 Se7 or 2 Sf4
   RxQ; 2 Se7
   BxQ; 2 Sf4
   KxS; 2 Sf4
   QxP ck; 2 SxQ
   QxQ; 2 Sh8

No. 41
1 Qh5

No. 42
1 Kb7, Sd8 ck; 2 Kb8, Sc6 ck; 3 Ka8, any; 4 Q or QS mates

No. 43
1 KRc2 threat 2 Rc3-d3
   Be5; 2 Ke3
   Be3; 2 Ke2
   Sf5; 2 Kg4
   Sf2; 2 KxS
   Pg4 ck; 2 KxB
   Rd6; 2 Se7

No. 44
1 Qa8, Pg3; 2 Q g2, any; 3 QxPg3
   Pe4; 2 Qa3, Pe3; 3 QxP
         Pg3; 3 QxP
   Ke5; 3 Qd6

The English composer, B. G. Laws, showed that by moving all the men one file to the left a different problem would result, the key then being 1 Qg1. Such similar positions are termed *twins*.

No. 45
1 Rg2, PxR; 2 QxP ck, Kg3; 3 Qh4
   Rf2; 2 Qe5 ck, Kf3; 3 Rg3
   Re3; 2 Qh4 ck, Kf3; 3 Rf2
   Rg3; 2 QxPd4 ck, Kf3; 3 Rf2
   Rf1; 2 Bg5 ck, Kf3; 3 Qa8

No. 46
1 Sd5, Pf5; 2 Rb1, PxP; 3 Sb6
   Bh7; 2 Ba7, BxP; 3 Se3

No. 47
1 Qd2 threat 2 Qh2
   Kd6; 2 Sc4

No. 48
    1 Be2, Kb7; 2 Qc8 ck, KxQ; 3 Ba6
           Kb6; 2 Qa5 ck, KxQ; 3 Bc7

No. 49
    1 Kg5 threat 2 Qf3 ck, Ke5; 3 Qf5
                Kd5; 2 Qf7 ck, Kc6; 3 KSd4
                Ke5; 2 Qe8 ck, Kd5; 3 Se3
                Kd3; 2 Qd1 ck, Kc4; 3 Sa3
                BxP; 2 Qe2 ck, Kd5; 3 SxS
                Pd5; 2 Qh7 ck, Ke5; 3 Qe7

No. 50
    1 Qe2, Kf5; 2 Kf7, Pe5; 3 Qf3
                      else; 3 Qe6
          Kg6; 2 Qf3, Kh7; 3 Qh5
                      else; 3 Qf7
          Pe5; 2 Qg4, Pe4; 3 Bb2
                    S any; 3 RxP
          Pe6; 2 Qh5, Pe5; 3 Qf7
                    else; 3 Qg5
          S any; 2 RxP ck etc.

No. 51
    1 Ra6 threat 2 Qf1
          RxB; 2 RxR
Jacobs shows this maneuver in a three-move setting in No. 138. Also compare No. 145 by Eaton.

No. 52
    1 Qh3, PxP; 2 Pb4 ck, PxP ep; 3 Qc3
                        Kc6; 3 Qc8
           KxP; 2 Qf5 ck, Kd4; 3 Pe3
           Kd4; 2 Be3 ck, KxP; 3 Qf5
                        Ke4,e5; 3 Qe6
          Pc3; 2 Qd3 etc.

No. 53
    1 Bh1, KxB; 2 Kf2, Ph3; 3 Kf1, Ph2; 4 Sf2
          Ph3; 2 Bg2, PxB; 3 Sf3 ck, Kf1; 4 Sh2
                                Kh1; 4 Sf2
               Ph2; 3 Se5, Ph1; 4 Se5-f3

No. 54
    1 Bh3, Pe4; 2 Qg4, any; 3 Qc8
          Pa5; 2 Qa6 ck, KxQ; 3 Bc8
          Kc7; 2 Qg4 etc.

This problem may be compared with Shinkman's No. 48. Problems with a total of seven or less men are termed *miniatures*.

Otto Wurzburg (1875-1951), a nephew of Shinkman, was one of the world's outstanding artists in problem composition. He was equally skilled in composing exquisite miniatures and in constructing highly strategic problems, all of his work being characterized by extreme polish.

Alain White, in the *Sketchbook,* writes: "Sharply pointed keys, brilliant sacrifices, mastery of difficult combinations, originality of idea, quiet play and beauty of mate, and astonishing economy of means, all of these abound in his delightful works."

No. 55
1 Qh7, SxQ; 2 SxS
        KxQS; 2 Sd3
        Ke5; 2 Sd3
        SxS ck; 2 KxS
        Se7 ck; 2 QxS

No. 56
1 Rb4, PxR; 2 Qb5 ck, RxQ; 3 Sc4
        Pc4; 2 Sb7 ck, KxR; 3 Qb1
        Rb6; 2 Qa6 ck, KxQ; 3 RxPa4
                RxQ; 3 Rb5
                KxR; 3 QxR

No. 57
1 Ka2 threat 2 Qh1 threat 3 Qb1
        Kf5; 2 QxB ck, KxQ; 3 Be6
                Ke4; 3 Qg6
        Be6; 2 Qg6 ck, Bf5; 3 Qc6

No. 58
1 Rg3 threat 2 Qc3 etc.
        Rb6; 2 Qc5 ck etc.
        Rg5; 2 Qf8 ck etc.

No. 59
1 Kd7, Kf4; 2 Ke6, any; 3 Sd5
        Pd2; 2 Qf3, Pd3; 3 Sc6

No. 60
1 Kc6, Sa5 ck; 2 Kb6, Sc4 ck; 3 Ka6, any; 4 Sc7
        Sd8 ck; 2 Kc7, Se6 ck; 3 Kc8, any; 4 Sb6

No. 61
   1 Re2, Pf4; 2 Ke1, Pf5; 3 Kf2, Kd3; 4 KRd2

No. 62
   1 QRd1, Pc6; 2 Rd6, Pg6; 3 Kf2, Kf5; 4 Ke3
           Pg6; 2 Rf6, Pc6; 3 Kd2, Kd5; 4 Ke3

No. 63
   1 Qg4 threat 2 Sd4
           Kb5; 2 Sc7
           Kd5; 2 Sg5
           Kd7; 2 SxPg7

No. 64
   1 Pd3
   A changed-mate waiter, or *mutate*, as such problems are
now termed, the key changing the set mates following
1 – – Sc3 and 1 – – Be3.

No. 65
   1 Rh2, KxP; 2 Bc6 ck, KxP; 3 Bc5
                       Ka5; 3 Rh5

No. 66
   1 Ke2, Pf1(Q) dbl ck; 2 Ke3 Q, B or R checks; 3 B or R
                                           captures the checking piece
           Pf1(S) dis ck; 2 Rf2 dis ck, KxS; 3 Bd3 or Pd3
           Sc1 ck; 2 Ke3 etc.
           Kd4; 2 Rf4 ck, Pe5; 3 SxB
           KxS; 2 Bd3 ck, Kd4; 3 Rf4
           Re7; 2 Rf7 dis ck etc.
   Compare this problem with No. 2 by Cook.

No. 67
   1 Ka8, Kd8; 2 Pe7 ck, Kc7; 3 Pe8(B), Kd8; 4 Se6

No. 68
   1 Qg1 threat 2 Bd4
           KxR; 2 Qg7
           SxR; 2 Qh2
           SxB; 2 Qa1
           QxP; 2 Rf5
           Rd5; 2 Sd7

No. 69
   1 Rg4 waiting

No. 70
>1 Rb7, Se5 ck; 2 Kc7, Sc4; 3 Rb1, any; 4 Ra1 ck etc.
>   Sd4 ck; 2 Kb6, Se6; 3 Rh7, any; 4 Rh8 ck etc.

No. 71
>1 Kc3, Se2 ck; 2 Kb4 etc.
>   Sd5 ck; 2 Kb3 etc.
>   Se4 ck; 2 Kc2 etc.
>   Sb5 ck; 2 Kd2 etc.

No. 72
>1 Pc8(S) threat 2 Pg4 ck, KxKS; 3 Qh8
>   BxS; 2 QSg4, any; 3 Qh7
>   Pg4; 2 Qh6, any; 3 Qf4

No. 73
>1 Rf3 threat 2 Rd3 ck, BxR; 3 PxB
>   QxP ck; 2 Ka2, QxQ ck; 3 Ra3
>   BxP ck; 2 Ka1 etc.
>   Qe3; 2 Rf2 dis ck etc.

Although Frederick Gamage (1882-1957) became most famous as a two-move composer, he also composed a number of three- and four-move problems in his earlier years.

No. 74
>1 Rg3 waiting

This is an illustration of a task, showing the queen giving mate on twelve different squares, the maximum possible.

About 1903 Joseph C. J. Wainwright (1851-1921) became interested in this task, which he christened the "Queen's Cross." An essay on it by him, with fifty examples by himself, Kennard and Gamage, was printed as an introductory essay to *Les Tours de Force sur l'Echiquier,* the 1906 volume of *The Christmas Series.*

No. 75
>1 Ra2, Sb6; 2 Ra6, any: 3 Qg4
>   Sc5; 2 Ra5, any; 3 Qf7

No. 76
>1 Qc1 threat 2 Sh6 ck, KxR; 3 Pd3
>   RxQ; 2 Rc4, any; 3 Sh6
>   RxP; 2 Pd4, RxR; 3 Sh6
>   KxR; 2 Pd3 ck, Kf5; 3 Sh6
>   Rf3; 2 PxR etc.

No. 77
  1 Se5 threat 2 Qb2 etc.
        QRd4; 2 Qd5, RxQ; 3 SxP
        KRd4; 2 Qe4, RxQ; 3 Sd7

The interference between two black rooks, where one moves along a rank and the other along a file, is termed a *Plachutta interference,* after a pioneer problem published in 1858 by Joseph Plachutta. In its original form a white piece was sacrificed on the *critical square,* which is the one where the movements of the rooks intersect; d4 in the present problem.

As Wurzburg shows, however, the sacrifice of a white man is not essential to the interference, and where there is no such sacrifice the maneuver is called a *Wurzburg-Plachutta.*

A black queen and bishop can make a similar interference when moving on intersecting diagonals. See problems 124, 178 and 182, which combine both forms of such interference.

No. 78
  1 Kc8 threat 2 Qg7 ck, Ke6; 3 Qf6
                        Kf4; 3 Bg5
        Pg2; 2 Pd4 ck, PxPep; 3 QxPe3

No. 79
  1 Pd3 threat 2 PxPe4

This problem was specifically composed to mislead the experienced solver, who would expect from the pawn arrangement that the composition featured en passant pawn captures by Black. Hence he would be led to believe that 1 Pd4, threatening 2 Sb6, was the key, especially since mates are set following en passant captures by either black pawn. 1 Pd4, however, is defeated by a single black move, 1 − − Bd8.

No. 80
  1 Be4 threat 2 QxP

This is a task problem, the white bishop being subject to capture by each of seven black men, each capture resulting in a different mate.

No. 81
  1 Rg1, Ph3; 2 KRe1, Kg4; 3 KRe4
        Pd3; 2 QRg5, Ke4; 3 KRg4

No. 82
  1 Rh8, Se8; 2 Rh7 etc.
        Sh5; 2 RxS etc.
        Kd6; 2 RxS etc.

No. 83
   1 Ra2, Bc7; 2 KRb2, Bb6; 3 RxB etc.
               Bd6; 2 KRc2, Bf4; 3 Ra1 ck etc.
               Be5; 2 KRd2, Bd4; 3 RxB etc.
               Bf4; 2 KRe2, Be3; 3 RxB etc.

No. 84
   1 Rf6, BxQR; 2 KxB etc.
            BxKR; 2 KxB etc.
            Bf8; 2 Rh8 ck etc.
            Bh8; 2 RxB ck etc.

No. 85
   1 Rg1, Ph1(B); 2 QRf1, PxR; 3 Rg8
          Ph1(Q); 2 Rg3 etc.
          Ph1(S); 2 Ra3 etc.

No. 86
   1 Ra6, Pf6; 2 Rg4, Pf5; 3 KRxP ck, KxR; 4 RxP
          Pf5; 2 Rg3, PxR ck; 3 Kg2, Kh4; 4 RxP

No. 87
   1 Pb8(B), Ke7; 2 Ph8(B), Kd8; 3 Bf6
                         Kf8; 3 Bd6

No. 88
   1 Rh4 waiting
             Pd6; 2 Qh8
             Pd5; 2 Qh3
   Since the publication of this famous problem, its strategic
theme, two interferences of a black pawn on a pinned black
queen allowing her to be unpinned in the ensuing mates, has
been called the *Gamage Theme.*

No. 89
   1 Qh6, Kd5; 2 Pc4 ck, PxPep; 3 SxP
            Kf5; 2 Pg4 ck, PxPep; 3 SxP

No. 90
   1 Kf3, SxSP ck; 2 Ke2 dis ck, Se4; 3 Qg8
          SxQP ck; 2 Kg4 dis ck, Se4; 3 Qa2

No. 91

Three consecutive promotions of pawns to bishops.

1 Ph8(B), RxS ck; 2 KPxR(B), Kd6; 3 Pc8(B), Kc5; 4 Be7
       Rf6; 2 BxR, Kd6; 3 Kb8, Kc5; 4 Sb7

This second continuation shows why the rook's pawn has to be promoted to a bishop; a queen would stalemate if it captured the rook. Similarly a promotion to queen on the second or the third move in the first continuation would result in stalemate.

No. 92

1 Rb7 threat 2 Qe7 ck, Kd5; 3 Rd7
       SxP; 2 Sb5 ck, Kc6; 3 Rc7
                    Ke6; 3 Re7
       Sc7; 2 PxS, Kd7; 3 Qd8
              else; 3 Pc8(S)

No. 93

1 Ke2, Ra1; 2 Be4 ck, Ka2; 3 Qg8
       Ra2 ck; 2 Bd2 dis ck, K any; 3 Qc1
       Re6 ck; 2 Be3 dis ck, K any; 3 Qc1
       Rf6; 2 Bf4 dis ck etc.
       Rg6; 2 Bg5 dis ck etc.
       Kc2; 2 Qd1 ck etc.
       Bb2; 2 Bd2 dis ck etc.

No. 94

1 Ra1, Pg5; 2 Ra4, Pg2; 3 Qe1
                  B any; 3 QxP
       Pg2; 2 Qf4, Pg5; 3 Qh2
       Kg5; 2 Sf3 ck etc.

Darso James Densmore (1867-1917), a son-in-law of Sam Loyd, composed some three hundred problems, the majority illustrating definite strategic themes, some of much complexity. Alain White devoted the 1920 volume of *The Christmas Series* to a collection of his problems and to positions contributed to a Densmore Memorial Tourney.

No. 95

1 Pd7, Kd6; 2 Pd8(S), PxB; 3 Rd7
       Kf7; 2 Pd8(Q) dis ck, Kg6; 3 Qg5
       PxP; 2 Pd8(R), Kf6; 3 Rd6
       PxB; 2 Pd8(B), Kd6; 3 Ra6

Compare this problem with No. 31.

No. 96
　　1 Pd6 threats 2 Sc6 ck and 3 Sf3 ck
　　　　　Kd5;　2 Sc6 threats 3 SxP and 3 Se3
　　　　　　　　KxS;　3 Be6
　　　　　KPxP;　2 SxSP threats 3 Sc6 and Sf3
　　　　　　　　KxS;　3 Bc3
　　　　　　　　PxS;　3 Pe3
　　　　　PxS;　2 Sf3 ck, Kd5;　3 Pe4

No. 97
　　1 Bd1, Pb4;　2 Ba4, any;　3 Bd7(x)
　　　　　Pd6;　2 Bb3, any;　3 QRe5
　　　　　Pg3;　2 Bh5, any;　3 Bf7(x)
　　　　　Pf6;　2 BxP, any;　3 KRe5

No. 98
　　1 Be1, K any;　2 Bc3, any;　3 Bb3
　　　　　Pa5;　2 Bb3, any;　3 Bc3

No. 99
　　1 Re2 threat 2 QxB ck, KxQ;　3 Rh2
　　　　　Qa2;　2 RxQ, Pg6;　3 Qb2
　　　　　QxB ck;　2 RxQ etc.
　　　　　Qe4;　2 RxQ etc.
　　　　　Qg2;　2 Se5 etc.

No. 100
　　1 KRg5 threat 2 Qh6
　　　　　　　Rc3;　2 Re3
　　　　　　　Rd4;　2 Re4
　　　　　　　R else;　2 Bc5(x)
　　　　　　　Sd4;　2 Re2
　　　　　　　Ph5;　2 Rg6

No. 101
　　1 Kf2, PxS;　2 Sc6 ck (threat), Kc8;　3 Rc7
　　　　　RxS;　2 PxR ck, K any;　3 Sd6
　　　　　Rf8;　2 Sc6 ck, Ke8;　3 Re7
　　　　　R else;　2 Pd7, PxS;　3 Sc6

　　Dr. Gilbert Dobbs (1867-1941), a Baptist minister, composed his first chess problem in 1900, and then throughout
the succeeding forty years produced over three thousand.
A selection of a hundred of his compositions was published
under the title *A Chess Silhouette* in 1942 as the fourth of the
series of problem books issued at Frank Altschul's private
Overbrook Press. Dr. Dobbs probably will best be remembered

for his many dainty lightweights, with their fine keys and attractive mating positions.

No. 102
1 Kd5, Sc3 ck;   2 Kc4, Rf4 ck;   3 Be4
       Se3 ck;   2 Kc5, Rf5 ck;   3 Bd5
       Sf4 ck;   2 Kd6, Rd3 ck;   3 Bd5
       Sf6 ck;   2 Ke6, Re3 ck;   3 Be4
       Rd3 ck;   2 Ke5 etc.
       Rf5 ck;   2 Kd4 etc.

No. 103
1 Kh2, QxR ck;   2 KSg3, QxB;   3 Se4
       Qe7;   2 Rd4, QxB;   3 Qb4
       Qb8;   2 QxQ, Kc4;   3 Rd4
       Qh7 ck;   2 Rh6 dis ck, Qe7;   3 BxQ

No. 104
1 Bh2, Pe3 ck;   2 Kg3, Ke5;   3 Sf3
       PxP;   2 Sf3 ck, Ke4;   3 Re6

No. 105
1 Kf4, Kd5;   2 Ke3, Ke6;   3 Kd4
       Pd5;   2 Kf5, KxS;   3 Ke5
A duel between kings; the white king discovering mate both from the rook and from the bishop. Problems in which the white king makes every move, at least in the main-play, have been termed *Durbars,* this being a typical example.

No. 106
1 Ke3 threat 2 BxR ck, QxB ck;   3 KxQ, any;   4 Pe5
       Kg6;   2 Pe5 dis ck, Rd3 dbl ck;   3 KxR etc.
                Re4 dbl ck;   3 KxR etc.

No. 107
1 Qc3 waiting
A mutate, six mates being changed by the key.

The Good Companion Chess Problem Club of Philadelphia owed its existence and outstanding success largely to its founder and secretary, James F. Magee, Jr. Although not a composer himself, Magee was interested in all forms of chess activities and in 1913 organized the Good Companion Club with ten charter members. Through the ensuing years it became international in scope, with its membership expanding to some six hundred problemists, including such world-famous two-move composers as Arnaldo Ellerman of

Argentina, Comins Mansfield of England and Giorgio
Guidelli of Italy.

The Club specialized in the study of the two-move problem,
holding monthly tourneys, with the honored problems published in its Folders. The Club finally dissolved in 1924.

Much of the work of the Club was classified and given a
permanent form in the 418-page 1922 volume of White's
Christmas Series, edited by George Hume and Alain White,
and entitled *The Good Companion Two-Mover.*

No. 108
> 1 Rc1, Pb5; 2 Pc5, Pb4; 3 BPxP ck, Kb5; 4 Pc4
>   Pc5; 2 Rd1, Pb5; 3 Rd5, Pb4; 4 RxP

No. 109
> 1 Bc1, KxP; 2 Be3, Kd5; 3 Bc6
>   Kf5; 3 Bg6
>   Kc5; 2 Bc6, Kb4; 3 Ba3
>   Kd4; 3 Be3

When two or more similar lines of play, or similar mating
positions, occur they are termed *echoes.* Where the black king
is thus mated on squares of different colors, they are *chame-
leon echoes.* Such echoes are shown in many other problems in
this volume. For typical examples see Nos. 97, 125, 126, 127,
141 and 147.

No. 110
> 1 Qa2, SxQ ck; 2 RxS, KxS; 3 Rd1
>   Se2 ck; 2 RxS etc.
>   S else; 2 Sf3 etc.

No. 111
> 1 Qa1, RxQ ck; 2 BxR, KxP; 3 RxP
>   Rf1; 2 Be8 etc.

No. 112
> 1 Rg8, Pg3; 2 Rh8, KxP; 3 Kg6
>   P any; 3 Kg7
>   PxP; 2 Kg7, Kg4; 3 Kh6

No. 113
> 1 Qc7, Bd7; 2 Kb1, B any; 3 Qg7
>   Kd4; 3 Sf3
>   Bf7; 2 Bh6, B any; 3 Qg7
>   Kf6; 3 Sg4
>   Kd4; 3 Sf3

No. 114
  1 Re8 waiting
        Sc5; 2 Sc3
        Sd4; 2 Re5
        Sc6; 2 BxQS
        Se6; 2 Se7

No. 115
  1 Rb4 waiting
        QxQ; 2 Be4
        Qd5; 2 Bb5
        Qd4; 2 Rb3
        Pe5; 2 Qh3
        B any; 2 Qh7

Alain White (1880-1951) was a skillful composer, but such ability was far overshadowed by his other activities in the chess problem field. In 1905 he published *Chess Lyrics, a Collection of Chess Problems by A. F. Mackenzie.* This became the first volume of the succeeding *Christmas Series* which White had printed and distributed each Christmas season to hundreds of problem composers and friends throughout the years to 1936, when the final volume, *A Genius of the Two-Mover,* a collection of Comins Mansfield's problems, concluded this delightful series. Some of these volumes were prepared entirely by White, while for others he had the collaboration of many prominent composers and problem lovers.

Another of White's outstanding contributions to the advancement of the chess problem art was his studies in the classification of themes that he began in 1908. This progressed to such a point that two years later he published the first fruits of his research in a series of articles in the *British Chess Magazine,* entitled *First Steps in the Classification of Two-Movers,* which he issued in book form in 1911. *The Good Companion Two-Mover* (1922) and *Simple Two-Move Themes* (1924) were more elaborate treatises on the classification of themes.

White's classified collection of problems continued to grow until after reaching more than two hundred thousand positions, it was moved to England in 1926 and George Hume undertook the arduous task of curator. Upon Hume's death in 1936 the collection was placed under the supervision of the British Chess Problem Society. It has since been divided into numerous sections; each in charge of an individual curator.

Then Alain White interested Frank Altschul in printing the beautiful series of problem books at Altschul's private *Overbrook Press,* that began with *A Century of Two-Movers,* issued in 1941, and included six other works, either edited by White or with his cooperation.

Yet undoubtedly Alain White's greatest contribution to chess problem art lay in his remarkable ability to enlist the enthusiastic cooperation of so many collaborators, both in this country and other lands. Although only meeting Alain White personally on a couple of occasions, the author owes a large debt to him for his encouragement in problem activities through a voluminous correspondence continuing over forty-odd years.

A sketch of his life, and of his other wide activities outside of the chess problem field, was written by Vincent L. Eaton (1915-1962) as an *Epilogue* to the second volume of *A Sketchbook of American Problematists.*

No. 116
>   1 Bc6, Qb5; 2 BxQ etc.
>   Qc3 ck; 2 KxQ etc.
>   Qe5 ck; 2 KxQ etc.
>   Q else; 2 K moves dis ck

No. 117
>   1 Qh8, KxB; 2 Sc3 ck, Ka1; 3 Qa8
>   Ka3; 3 Qf8
>   PxB; 2 Sd4, Pb1(Q) ck; 3 Sb3
>   Kb1; 3 Qh1

No. 118
>   1 Sf4 waiting
>   A mutate.

No. 119
>   1 Qe3 threat 2 Pc4

A block-threat, the initial waiting move position being changed by the key.

No. 120
>   1 Qc7, Sd7; 2 Qc4
>   QS else; 2 Qc8(x)
>   KS any; 2 Pd5

Where two black men are on a line between the black king and a long range white piece—queen, rook or bishop—and there are no other intervening men, the black men are said to be *half-pinned*. Either is free to move off the line, but if it does the other black man will become pinned. Any resulting mate, which the pinned black man could otherwise prevent, is known as a *pin-mate*.

Such half-pinning is shown most economically in this constructional gem, where the two black knights are half-pinned by the white rook.

The problem is a mutate with typical changed-mate play. Before the key if 1 – – Sd7 White could mate by 2 Qg8, and if 1 – – KS any by 2 Qd5, both of which are pin-mates. After the keymove, 1 Qc7, these are replaced by different pin-mates.

No. 121

          1 Rd7, KxR;   2 PxR(S)
                    SxR;   2 PxR(Q)
                    KxB;   2 Pc8(S)
                    Se6;   2 Pc8(Q)
                    Rc8;   2 PxS(S)
                    Kc8;   2 PxS(Q)

Threefold promotions to knight and to queen on the mating moves. This position is an improved version of an earlier problem entered by Bettman in *La Stratégie* tourney, 1908-1910.

No. 122

          1 Rf6, Sh3;   2 RxP (threat), PxR;   3 RxS
                              Sg5;   3 Rg8
                    Ph5;   3 KRxP ck, PxR;   3 Rh6

No. 123

          1 Ra3, PxP;   2 Rb3, Pc2;   3 KRxP, Pc1;   4 Rh3
                    Pc2;   2 Kf5, KxP;   3 Rh3 ck, PxR;   4 RxP
                    Pc4;   2 QRxP, P(either)x R;   3 RxP, Pg3;   4 RxPc4(d4)
                    Pg3;   2 Re3, PxR;   3 RxP, Kg4;   4 Rc4

No. 124

          1 Pc5 threat 2 Pc6
                    QRd6;   2 QxQP ck, RxQ;   3 Se6
                    KRd6;   2 Se6 ck, RxS;   3 QxQP
                    Be4;   2 RxBP ck, BxR;   3 QxBP
                    Qe4;   2 QxBP ck, QxQ;   3 RxBP
                    Qd3;   2 QxQP ck, QxQ;   3 RxBP

The threat, 2 Pc6, sets up an interference on the black queen's rook and bishop, with third-move mating threats of 3 Se6 and 3 QxBP. This is known as a *Nowotny inter-ference*. To avoid these threatened mating moves, either the rook or bishop must move across the critical square, c6, or black must make some other move that will make one or the other threat inoperative. Such moves lead to *Plachutta inter-ferences*. Compare this problem with No. 77, No. 178 and No. 182.

No. 125

```
1 Qh1, SxS;  2 Qb7 ck, Kc5;  3 Se4 ck, Kc4;  4 Pb3
                        Ka5;  3 Sc4 ck, Ka4;  4 Pb3
                        Ka4;  3 Pb3 ck; Ka3;  4 Sc4
          PxS;  2 Qb7 ck, Kc4;  3 Se5 ck, Kc5;  4 Pb4
          Kb6;  2 Sc4 ck, Kb5;  3 Qd5 ck, Ka4;  4 Sb6
```

No. 126

```
1 PxP, Pg5;  2 Rh3 ck, Ke4;  3 Rf3, Pg4;  4 Pd3
                        Kc4;  3 Rb3, Pg4;  4 Pd3
       Kc4;  2 Pd5 dis ck, Kc5;  3 Rb4, Pg5;  4 Pd4
                          Kb5;  3 Rb4 ck, Kc5;  4 Pd4
                                   K else;  4 Ra8
                          Kd3;  3 Rc8, any;  4 Rc3
       Kc2;  2 Rb8, Kd3;  3 Rc8, Pg5;  4 Rc3
                  else;  3 Rh3, any;  4 Rc3
```

No. 127

```
1 Ka8, Pa2;  2 Ba7 threat 3 Qh3
                  Kg3;  3 Qf2
       Pe4;  2 Ba6, any;  3 Qf1
```

No. 128

```
1 Rb7, Kd5;  2 Sd8, Kc5;  3 Be5, Kd5;  4 Rb5
                  Kd6;  3 Bd4, Kd5;  4 Rd7
       Kf5;  2 Rb6, Kf4;  3 Kf2, Kf5;  4 Rf6
```

No. 129

```
1 Qg1 threat 2 Qg4 etc.
       0-0-0;  2 Qa7, SxQ;  3 RxP
       Rd8;  2 Qd4, SxQ;  3 SxP
```

No. 130

```
1 Ba1 threat 2 Kg7 and 3 Bf6
       PxP;  2 Sc3, any;  3 Sd5(x)
```

No. 131
    1 Kh2 threat 2 Sh1
            Pc6; 2 Se5
            Pc5; 2 Sd6
            BxP; 2 SxB
            Pe1(Q); 2 Rg2
            Pe1(S); 2 Rf1

No. 132
    1 Qh8, Ke3; 2 Qb2, KxS; 3 Qc3
                        Kf3; 3 Qe2
            Kg2; 2 Se1 ck, Kg1; 3 Bb6
                            Kf2; 3 Qd4
            Pb2; Bb6, Kg2; 3 Se1

No. 133
    1 Rb8, QxQP; 2 Pf8(S) (threat)
            QxKP; 2 Pf8(S)
            QxBP; 2 Pe8(Q)
            KxP; 2 Pf8(Q)
            Sd8; 2 PxS(Q)
            Sc8; 2 RxSb7

No. 134
    1 Qe1, Kc7; 2 Qb4, Kc8; 3 Qb8
            else; 2 Qa5 etc.

No. 135
    1 Qd7 threat 2 Sb3 ck, KxS; 3 Qf5
            Pe6; 2 Sb3 ck, KxS; 3 Qh7
            PxS(Q); 2 Sb3 ck, Ka2; 3 Qa4
            PxS(S); 2 Sc2 ck, Ka2; 3 QxPd5
            KxS; 2 Qf5 ck, Ka1; 3 Sb3

No. 136
    1 Sd4, Kh6; 2 Se2, Kh5; 3 SxP ck, Kh4; 4 Pg3
                        Pf3; 3 Sf4, PxP; 4 Rg6
            Pf3; 2 Pg3, any; 3 Sf5, any; 4 Pg4
            Kh4; 2 Sf3 ck, Kh5; 3 Kh7, any: 4 Rg5

No. 137
    1 Re6 threat 2 Ra6
            Bf5; 2 Bf8
            Bc2; 2 Bc1

No. 138
    1 Rc7 threat 2 Qc4
            Sf6; 2 QxP ck, RxQ; 3 RxR
                          KxQ; 3 Rc4
            RxR; 2 Qb5 threats 3 Qd3 and Qd5
            Sa6; 2 Qc6 ck etc.

No. 139
    1 Ra4, Kf5; 2 Ra5, any; 3 Sd6
            Kd5; 2 Ra5 ck, Ke4; 3 Sd6
            Pd3; 2 Se3 dis ck, KxSe5; 3 Bf4

No. 140
    1 Sd4 waiting. A mutate.

No. 141
    1 Rg1 threat 2 QxP ck, Kh5; 3 Pg4
            Kh5; 2 Q g4 ck, Kh4; 3 Pg3

No. 142
    1 Bh5 waiting
            Bd2; 2 Pe3
            Sc2; 2 Pe4

No. 143
    1 Se5 threat 2 Sd7 ck, Ka5; 3 Be1
            Ka5; 2 Be1 ck, Kb6; 3 Sd7
            Kc5; 2 Sd3 ck, Kb6; 3 Bc7
            Pe6; 2 KSc4 ck, Kc5; 3 Bd6
            Pd3; 2 Bf2 ck, Ka5; 3 Sc6
            Be6; 2 Sd3, Ka5; 3 Bc7

No. 144
    1 Sc8-d6 threat 2 QxB ck, Qf7; 3 RxP
                    KxR dis ck; 2 Sf7 dis ck, Ke6; 3 Sd8
                    Ke5 dis ck; 2 Pf7 dis ck, Ke6; 3 Pf8(S)
                    Qe8; 2 SxP ck, KxR dis ck; 3 Sd6-f7
                                   Ke5 dis ck; 3 Sd6-f7
                    Q g6; 2 Sb7, Kf7; 3 RxP
                    Rf7; 2 Sb7 etc.
                    PxP; 2 Sf7 etc.

No. 145
    1 Rb3 threat 2 KRe3
            Rf4; 2 Rb5
            Kf4 dis ck; 2 KRc3
            Sf4; 2 Sf3
            Pf4; 2 RxP

No. 146
  1 Pb8(S), RxP ck; 2 Kc7, any; 3 Sc6 or Sd7
       Re7; 2 PxR, Kd6; 3 Qd4
       Re8 ck; 2 KxR, KxP; 3 Qe7
       Rg6; 2 Qe4 ck, any; 3 Qe7
       Rh6; 2 Sd7 ck, KxP; 3 QxR

No. 147
  1 Bf5, Kf1; 2 Bg4, Kf2; 3 Bd2, Kg3; 4 Be1
              Kf1; 4 Rf4
       Kf3; 2 Kg1, Ke2; 3 Bc2, Kf3; 4 Bd1
              Ke1; 4 Re4
       Ke2; 2 Kg2, Ke1; 3 Bd3, Kd1; 4 Ra1
       Ke1; 2 Bg4, Kf1; 2 Be3, Ke1; 4 Ra1

No. 148
  1 Ba6 threat 2 Se2 ck, KxS; 3 Bd3
       Bc5 ck; 2 Kb5 dis ck, Kd3; 3 Kc6
              Bb4 dis ck; 3 Qd5
       Sc5; 2 Ka5 dis ck, SxR dis ck; 3 Qd5
       QxP; 2 Ka3 dis ck, Ke3; 3 Sd5

No. 149
  1 KSd6, Kd5; 2 Rh5 ck, Be5; 3 Sc3
            Qe5; 3 Sf6
      Qg8; 2 Ra5 ck, Bd5; 3 Sc4
            Qd5; 3 Sf7

No. 150
  1 Sc2 threat 2 Sb4
       Kd3; 2 Sf2 ck, Kd2; 3 Be3 ck, Ke2; 4 Bd3
              Ke2; 3 Bd3 ck, Kd2; 4 Be3
              Kc4; 3 Sd3, Kd5; 4 Se3
       Kd5; 2 Se3 ck, Ke5; 3 Sf2, BxPg3; 4 Sd3
              BxPg5; 4 Sg4

No. 151
  1 Pd4 threat 2 Pd5 ck, PxP; 3 KBxP
       BPxPep; 2 Qa2 ck, Pd5; 3 BPxPep
       KPxPep; 2 Pf4 threat 3 Pf5
              Pf5; 3 PxPep

No. 152
  1 Pc6 threat 2 Re8 ck etc.
       Qe7 ck; 2 Pg5 dis ck, Pf5; 3 PxPep
       Qd6; 2 Re8 ck, Kd5; 3 Re5

No. 153
 1 Rc8, Pd5; 2 Bc7, Kc5; 3 Be5
   else; 2 Bf5, any; 3 Rd3

No. 154
 1 Qh1 threat 2 Rd2 ck, RxR; 3 Qa8
    RxQ; 2 Ra2, any; 3 Ra8
    SxR; 2 Qa1 etc.
    RxR; 2 Qh4 ck etc.
    Ke8; 2 Re2 ck etc.
    Bg5; 2 RxR etc.

No. 155
 1 Rh1, Kg4; 2 Kh2, Kh5; 3 Kg3
    Pg4; 2 Sh2, K any; 3 Sf1

No. 156
 1 Ra8 waiting. A mutate.

No. 157
 1 Bg8 waiting
 A mutate where the black king by its moves self-pins black
pieces three times.

No. 158
 1 Qb6 threat 2 Sf2 dis ck, Kg5; 3 Qd8
    Ke4: 2 Qe3 ck, PxQ; 3 KSe5
    Pg5; 2 Qg6 ck, KxQ; 3 KSe5
    Qd3; 2 Se3 dbl ck, Ke4; 3 Bg2
    Qe4; 2 KSe5 dis ck, Kg5; 3 Qd8

No. 159
 1 Kg2, Se3 ck; 2 RxS ck, KxR dis ck; 3 Sf3
            KxKS dis ck; 3 Sc6
    Qa2 ck; 2 QSe2 dis ck, QxR; 3 Sg3
    Pd5; 2 Qe7 ck, Se6; 3 QxS

No. 160
 1 Ka2 threat 2 Qb3
    Qa3 ck; 2 QxQ
    Qa5; 2 QxQ
    Qa7; 2 Sd5
    Qb4; 2 Qc2
    Qb5; 2 Qd4
    Qc4 ck; 2 QxQ
    Qd5 ck; 2 SxQ

No. 161
```
1 Qa5, KxS;  2 Bd1
        Kb1;  2 Bg6
        Pb1(S);  2 Qa2
        Pb1(else);  2 Qc3
```

No. 162
```
1 Qb1 threat 2 Qc1
        Bd7;  2 Sc4
        Bc4;  2 Sf7
        Sc4;  2 Rd3
        RxPa3;  2 Sg6
        RxPg4 ck;  2 SxR
```

No. 163
```
1 Sd7 waiting
    Qf4;  2 Rc3
    Qe3;  2 Rc3
    Rd3;  2 Rc3
    Re4;  2 Rc4
    Rf4;  2 Qh6
    Ra4;  2 Qh6
    Rd5;  2 Rc6
```

No. 164
```
1 Qf4, Ra1;  2 Bb4 (threat), KxP;  3 Sc3
        Pd5;  2 Bb4 (threat), KxP;  3 Sd6
        Ra4;  2 Sc3 dis ck, KxSc5;  3 SxR
        Sa6;  2 Sf6 dis ck;  KxS;  3 SxP
        KxP;  2 Sf6 dis ck, KxS;  3 Qb4
        Bh2;  2 QxP ck, KxQ;  3 Bf2
        Sb6, e7;  2 Qe5 ck, KxQ;  3 Bc3
                        KxP;  3 Sd6
```

No. 165
```
1 Rf5, Ka2;  2 Ra5 ck, Kb1;  3 Qf5
                      Ba3;  3 Qb2
        Ba3;  2 Rf1 ck, Ka2;  3 QxP
                      Bc1;  3 Qb2
        Kc2;  2 Rb5 etc.
```

No. 166
```
1 Qb1 threat 2 Qb4
        QxR;  2 Pc3
        Qb3;  2 PxQ
        Qd3;  2 PxQ
        Qe5, g5;  2 Pc4
```

In the initial position of this remarkable problem if the black queen moves, White's king's knight's pawn can effect four similar mates: 1 — — Qh3; 2 PxQ: 1 — — Qf3; 2 PxQ: 1 — — QxS; 2 Pg3: 1 — — Qg5; 2 Pg4. The key transfers such mating play from the pawn on g2 to the one on c2.

No. 167
　　1 Rf4 waiting

No. 168
　　1 Rg5 threat 2 BxQ threat 3 Qe1
　　　　　　Sd3;　2 Sc2 ck, BxS;　3 Qc3
　　　　　　Se4;　2 Sd3 ck, QxS;　3 QxB
　　　　　　Sd6;　2 Sc6 ck, RxS;　3 Qc3
　　　　　　Bb6;　2 SxP ck, RxS;　3 Qb5

No. 169
　　1 Qd1, KxPc5;　2 Qb1, Kd5;　3 Qe1, Kc5;　4 Qa5
　　　　　　　　　　　　　　　　　　　　Pc5;　4 Qe4
　　　　KxPe5;　2 Qf1, Kd5;　3 Qc1, Ke5;　4 Qg5
　　　　　　　　　　　　　　　　　　　　Pe5;　4 Qc4

No. 170
　　1 Kg2 threat 2 Qd3 threat 3 Qd7
　　　　　　　　　　　Sd5;　3 Qh3
　　　　　　Se4;　2 Qb3 ck, Kf5;　3 Qh3
　　　　　　QS else;　2 Qg4 ck, Kd5;　3 Pc4
　　　　　　KS any;　2 Qc6(x) ck, Kf5;　3 Bd7

No. 171
　　1 Ra2, Qc7, h2;　2 Ra8 ck etc.
　　　　Qc8, g8;　2 Rh2 ck etc.

No. 172
　　1 Qh6, Pf4;　2 QxP ck (threat), RxQ;　3 SxP
　　　　　　Bh5, h7;　2 Qc6 ck, Qd5;　3 QxQ
　　　　　　Bf7;　2 Qh1, any;　3 Qb1

No. 173
　　1 Rf7 threat 2 RxP ck, KxR;　3 Qh5
　　　　　　Sd6;　2 QxP ck, KxQ;　3 Re7
　　　　　　Bb2;　2 Qb8 ck, Sd6;　3 QxKB
　　　　　　Bc1;　2 Qb5 ck, Sc5;　3 Qb8
　　　　　　　　　　　　　　Kd6;　3 Rd7
　　　　　　Kd6;　2 Qd7 ck etc.

No. 174
    1 Ke4 threat 2 Qg3 ck, Kd1; 3 KSe3
            Rg1; 2 Qc3 ck, Kf1; 3 QSe3
            Kd1; 2 KSe3 ck, Ke1; 3 Qg3
            Kf1; 2 QSe3 ck, Ke1; 3 Qc3

No. 175
    1 Bg1 threat 2 Bh2
            Kg3; 2 Rg5
            Re4; 2 Rf5
            Rd3; 2 Rd5
            Rc3; 2 Rc5
            Qb3; 2 Re4

No. 176
    1 Sa5, Kc5; 2 Rd7, Re2; 3 Rd5
            Kd4; 2 Rf5, R moves; 3 Rd5
            Kd6; 2 Rb5 etc.
            Ke5; 2 Rd3 etc.

No. 177
    1 Pb8(R), Bf2; 2 BxB, Kh2; 3 Rh8
                 Bb4; 2 RxB, Kg1; 3 Rb1
                 BxB; 2 KxB, Kg1; 3 Rb1

No. 178
    1 Bg2 threat 2 QxPe5 ck, PxQ; 3 QBxP
            Qb5; 2 Se2 ck, QxS; 3 Sc6
            Bb5; 2 Sc6 ck, BxS; 3 Se2
            QRf6; 2 Se6 ck, QRxS; 3 SxP
            KRf6; 2 SxP ck, KRxS; 3 Se6

No. 179
    1 Qc2 threat 2 Qh7
            RxRg7; 2 QxR

No. 180
    1 Kd7, BxB; 2 Qa8 etc.
            Rg3; 2 BxR dis ck etc.
            Rg4; 2 Bf4 dis ck, Rh4; 3 Qa8
            Rg7 ck; 2 QxR etc.

No. 181
    1 Pg8(R) threat 2 RxR etc.
                RxR; 2 PxR(R) etc.
                Re5 ck; 2 PxR etc.
                Re2; 2 QxR etc.

No. 182

 1 Rd5 threat 2 Re5 ck, PxR; 3 QxP
   Bb4; 2 SxPc5 ck, BxS; 3 Sc3
   Qb4; 2 Sc3 ck, QxS; 3 SxPc5
   QRg2; 2 SxPf2 ck, RxS; 3 Sg3
   KRg2; 2 Sg3 ck, RxS; 3 SxPf2

In each of the four thematic variations Black defeats the threat by unpinning one of the black knights, by moving another piece onto the line of pin, thus combining unpinning with the *Plachutta interferences.*

No. 183

 1 Qc7 threat 2 QxP
   Se4; 2 Sg4
   Sf5; 2 Qe5
   S else; 2 Rh3

The key changes three mates following moves of the black knight.

No. 184

 1 KxP threats 2 Qe7 ck and 2 Se7 ck
   Rb7 ck; 2 Ke6, Rb6 ck; 3 Sd6
         Re7 ck; 3 SxR
   Bc6 ck; 2 Kd6, Bh2 ck; 3 Sg3
         Rd4 ck; 3 KSxR

No. 185

 1 Bh8, Kg4; 2 Sh5 dis ck, Kf5; 3 Sg7
          KxSh3; 3 QxPd7
          KxSh5; 3 Qd1
   QP any; 2 Sf2 etc.
   else; 2 QxP ck etc.

No. 186

 1 Re7, RxR; 2 QxPh7 ck (threat), KxS; 3 Qh2
   BxR; 2 Be6 ck (threat), KxS; 3 Qf1
   SxS; 2 Qb1, SxQ; 3 Be6

This last variation is the "heart" of the problem.

No. 187

 1 Rc6 threat 2 QxP ck, KRxQ; 3 Rc8
         QRxQ; 3 RxPa6
         KxQ; 3 RxPc5
   PxR; 2 QxP ck, KRb7; 3 Qc8
         QRb7; 3 QxPa6
   Pb6 ck; 2 RxPb6 dis ck etc.

No. 188
    1 Se4, Sc3; 2 Sg3 etc.
          Sg3; 2 Sc3 etc.
          Sc1, f4; 2 Rd2 etc.
          Sg1, d4; 2 Rf2 etc.

No. 189
    1 Re6 threat 2 Rf6 ck, KxS; 3 Bf3
              KxS; 2 Rd4 ck, Kf5; 3 Bg4
              KxR; 2 Bg4 ck, KxR; 3 Qb7
                                      Ke7; 3 Qc7
              RxR; 2 Qb1, KxS; 3 Sb4
                          else; 3 Sd4

Here again this last variation is the "heart" of the problem.

No. 190
    1 Rh2, Rh1; 2 Ke7 etc.
            Re1 ck; 2 Be5 dis ck etc.
            Rd6 ck; 2 BxR dis ck etc.

No. 191
    1 Qa7 waiting
                Pd6; 2 Qe3 ck, Kd5; 3 Rf5
                Pd5; 2 Qe7 ck, Kd4; 3 Qe3
                Ke6; 2 Qd4, Pd6; 3 Qe4
                              else; 3 Qf6
              Ke4; 2 Qc5 etc.
              K else; 2 Rf5 etc.

No. 192
    1 Kb7 waiting
              Pc6; 2 KxP, PxS; 3 Kd5
              Pc5; 2 Rd2, PxS; 3 RxP
              PxS; 2 RxP ck, Kd4; 3 Bb2

No. 193
    1 Qg1 threat 2 Qa7 ck, Kb4; 3 Sd5
              Ka3; 2 Qa1 ck, Kb4; 3 Sa6
              Kb4; 2 Sd5 ck, Ka3; 3 Qa1
                        Ka4, a5; 3 Qa7
              Bc5; 2 QxB, Pb4; 3 Qa7
              Bb4; 2 Qd4 etc.

No. 194
>   1 Kb3 waiting
>>   Pc4 ck;   2 Ka4, Ka7;   3 Kb5
>>   else;   3 Qf2
>>   PxS;   2 KxP, Kc6;   3 Qe6
>>   Kb5;   2 Qa4 ck, Kb6;   3 Sd5

No. 195
>   1 Bb1 waiting
>>   Kb3, a3;   2 Sc2(ck), any;   3 Rb4
>>   KxB;   2 Bc3, any;   3 Rf1
>>   Pg3;   2 Bc2, Ka1;   3 Bc3
>>   Ka3;   3 Bc1

No. 196
>   1 Qa3 waiting
>>   Kd2;   2 QxS ck, Ke1;   3 Sd3
>>   Sd1;   2 Bd3 ck, Kd2;   3 Sf3
>>   Kb1;   2 Sc4, SxS;   3 Bd3
>>   Sd3;   2 SxS etc.
>>   S else;   2 Sc4 etc.

No. 197
>   1 Bc4 threat 2 RxP dis ck
>>   QxB ck;   2 Kh8 threat 3 Rg8
>>   Pe4;   3 Rh1
>>   SxB;   2 BxP, any;   3 Bg5
>>   Pe4;   2 SxPf5 ck, Kh5;   3 BxPe2

No. 198
>   1 Pe8(B) waiting
>>   Sa7;   2 Qd6 ck, Ka8;   3 SxP
>>   Sd6;   2 KxS, Kc8;   3 Qa8
>>   Se7;   2 SxS, Kc7;   3 Qd6
> The initial position is a complete block and a keymove must be found that will not disturb it.

No. 199
>   1 Bc1 threat 2 Bb2 ck, Ke3;   3 Sd5
>>   Pc4;   2 Qf5 threat 3 Sb5
>>   Pc3;   3 Qd5
>>   Pf2;   2 Qe2 etc.
>>   Ke5;   2 QxPc5 ck etc.

No. 200
    1 Sf4 threat 2 Sh6
        Pe3 dis ck; 2 Sd5
        BxS; 2 RxB
        KxSf5; 2 Be6
        SxS; 2 Bh5

The *American Chess Bulletin* was founded by Hermann Helms (1870-1963) sixty years ago and during its earlier years its problem department was in charge of Henry W. Barry (1878-1932). From 1935 through 1948 it was edited by the author and since that time it had been conducted by Edgar Holladay until the publication of the *Bulletin* was discontinued after Helms' death.

Index of Composers

THE FIGURES REFER TO PROBLEM NUMBERS

A CATALOGUE OF SELECTED DOVER
BOOKS IN ALL FIELDS OF INTEREST

CONDITIONED REFLEXES, Ivan P. Pavlov. Full translation of most complete statement of Pavlov's work; cerebral damage, conditioned reflex, experiments with dogs, sleep, similar topics of great importance. 430pp. 5⅜ x 8½. 60614-7 Pa. $4.50

NOTES ON NURSING: WHAT IT IS, AND WHAT IT IS NOT, Florence Nightingale. Outspoken writings by founder of modern nursing. When first published (1860) it played an important role in much needed revolution in nursing. Still stimulating. 140pp. 5⅜ x 8½. 22340-X Pa. $3.00

HARTER'S PICTURE ARCHIVE FOR COLLAGE AND ILLUSTRATION, Jim Harter. Over 300 authentic, rare 19th-century engravings selected by noted collagist for artists, designers, decoupeurs, etc. Machines, people, animals, etc., printed one side of page. 25 scene plates for backgrounds. 6 collages by Harter, Satty, Singer, Evans. Introduction. 192pp. 8⅞ x 11¾. 23659-5 Pa. $5.00

MANUAL OF TRADITIONAL WOOD CARVING, edited by Paul N. Hasluck. Possibly the best book in English on the craft of wood carving. Practical instructions, along with 1,146 working drawings and photographic illustrations. Formerly titled *Cassell's Wood Carving*. 576pp. 6½ x 9¼.
23489-4 Pa. $7.95

THE PRINCIPLES AND PRACTICE OF HAND OR SIMPLE TURNING, John Jacob Holtzapffel. Full coverage of basic lathe techniques—history and development, special apparatus, softwood turning, hardwood turning, metal turning. Many projects—billiard ball, works formed within a sphere, egg cups, ash trays, vases, jardiniers, others—included. 1881 edition. 800 illustrations. 592pp. 6⅛ x 9¼. 23365-0 Clothbd. $15.00

THE JOY OF HANDWEAVING, Osma Tod. Only book you need for hand weaving. Fundamentals, threads, weaves, plus numerous projects for small board-loom, two-harness, tapestry, laid-in, four-harness weaving and more. Over 160 illustrations. 2nd revised edition. 352pp. 6½ x 9¼.
23458-4 Pa. $6.00

THE BOOK OF WOOD CARVING, Charles Marshall Sayers. Still finest book for beginning student in wood sculpture. Noted teacher, craftsman discusses fundamentals, technique; gives 34 designs, over 34 projects for panels, bookends, mirrors, etc. "Absolutely first-rate"—E. J. Tangerman. 33 photos. 118pp. 7¾ x 10⅝. 23654-4 Pa. $3.50

AMERICAN ANTIQUE FURNITURE, Edgar G. Miller, Jr. The basic coverage of all American furniture before 1840: chapters per item chronologically cover all types of furniture, with more than 2100 photos. Total of 1106pp. 7⅞ x 10¾.   21599-7, 21600-4 Pa., Two-vol. set $17.90

ILLUSTRATED GUIDE TO SHAKER FURNITURE, Robert Meader. Director, Shaker Museum, Old Chatham, presents up-to-date coverage of all furniture and appurtenances, with much on local styles not available elsewhere. 235 photos. 146pp. 9 x 12.   22819-3 Pa. $6.00

ORIENTAL RUGS, ANTIQUE AND MODERN, Walter A. Hawley. Persia, Turkey, Caucasus, Central Asia, China, other traditions. Best general survey of all aspects: styles and periods, manufacture, uses, symbols and their interpretation, and identification. 96 illustrations, 11 in color. 320pp. 6⅛ x 9¼.   22366-3 Pa. $6.95

CHINESE POTTERY AND PORCELAIN, R. L. Hobson. Detailed descriptions and analyses by former Keeper of the Department of Oriental Antiquities and Ethnography at the British Museum. Covers hundreds of pieces from primitive times to 1915. Still the standard text for most periods. 136 plates, 40 in full color. Total of 750pp. 5⅜ x 8½.
23253-0 Pa. $10.00

THE WARES OF THE MING DYNASTY, R. L. Hobson. Foremost scholar examines and illustrates many varieties of Ming (1368-1644). Famous blue and white, polychrome, lesser-known styles and shapes. 117 illustrations, 9 full color, of outstanding pieces. Total of 263pp. 6⅛ x 9¼. (Available in U.S. only)   23652-8 Pa. $6.00

Prices subject to change without notice.

Available at your book dealer or write for free catalogue to Dept. GI, Dover Publications, Inc., 180 Varick St., N.Y., N.Y. 10014. Dover publishes more than 175 books each year on science, elementary and advanced mathematics, biology, music, art, literary history, social sciences and other areas.